T

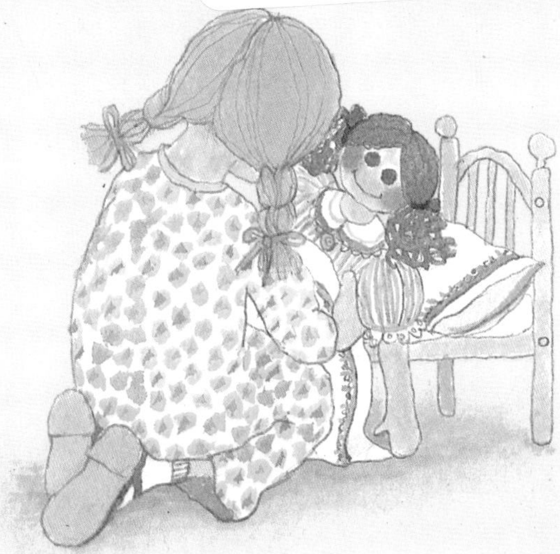

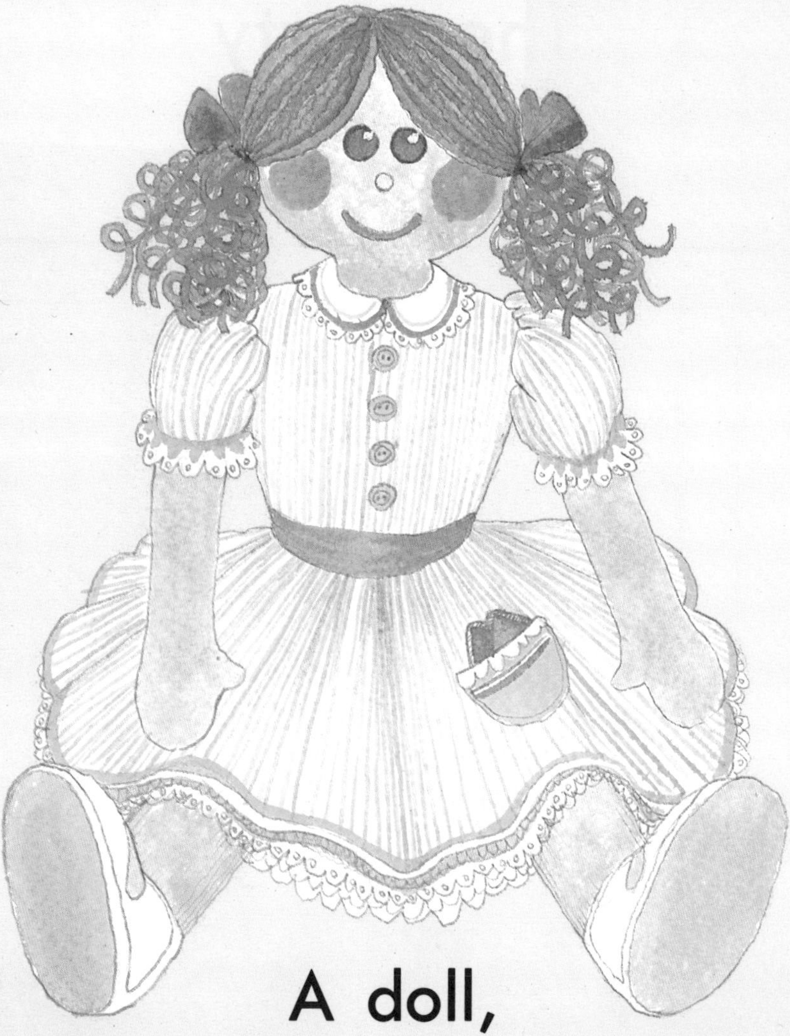

A doll,

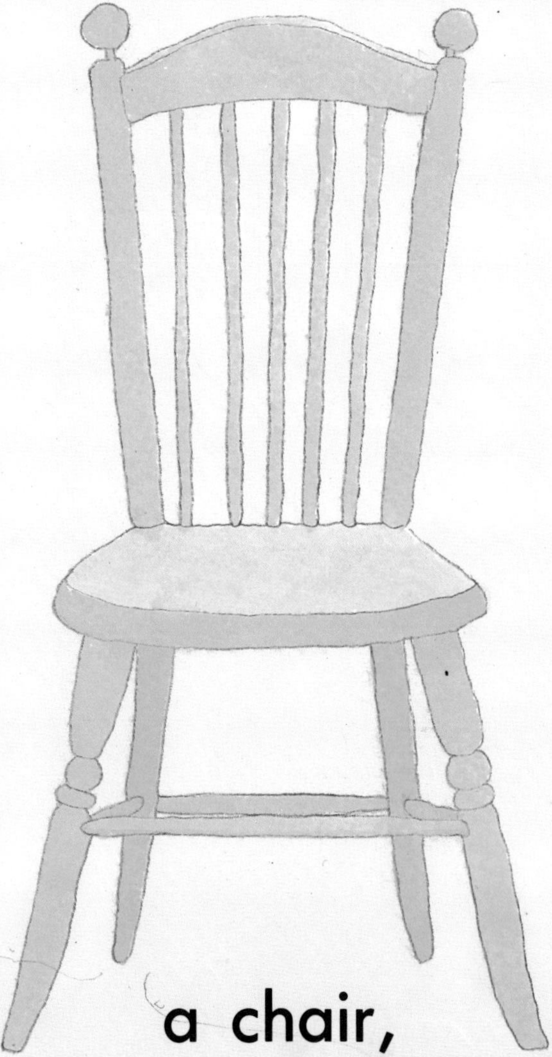

a chair,

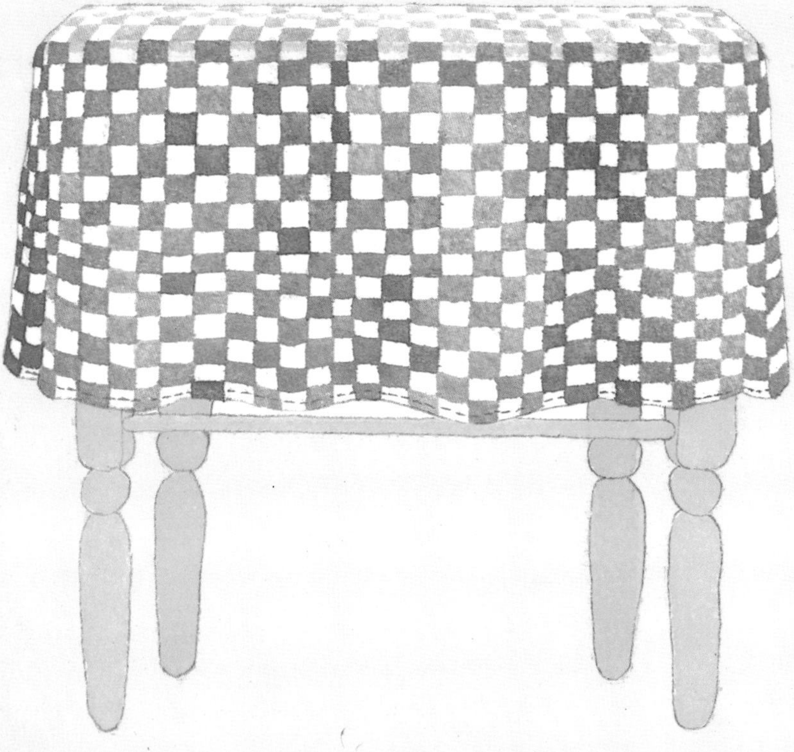

a table,

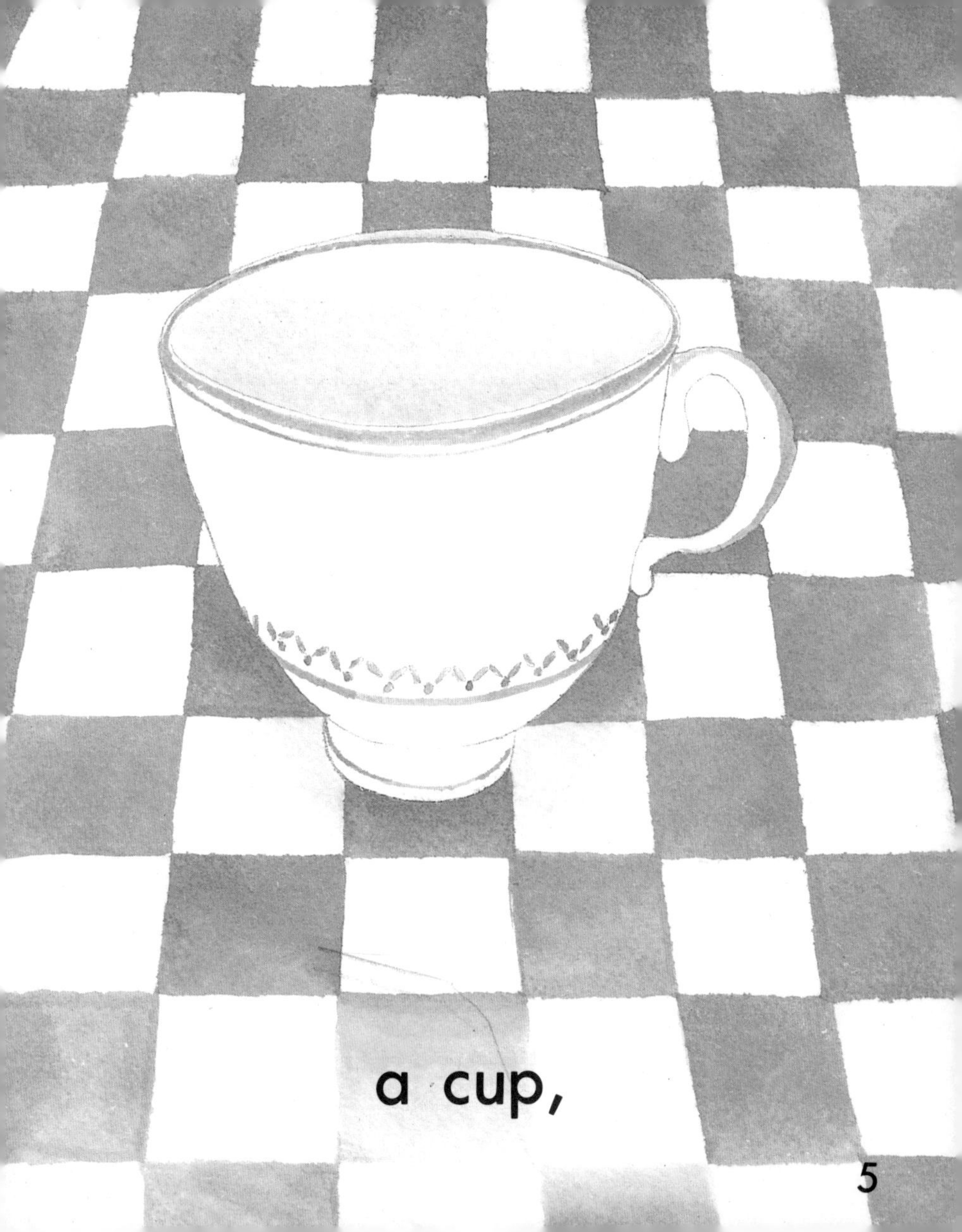

a cup,

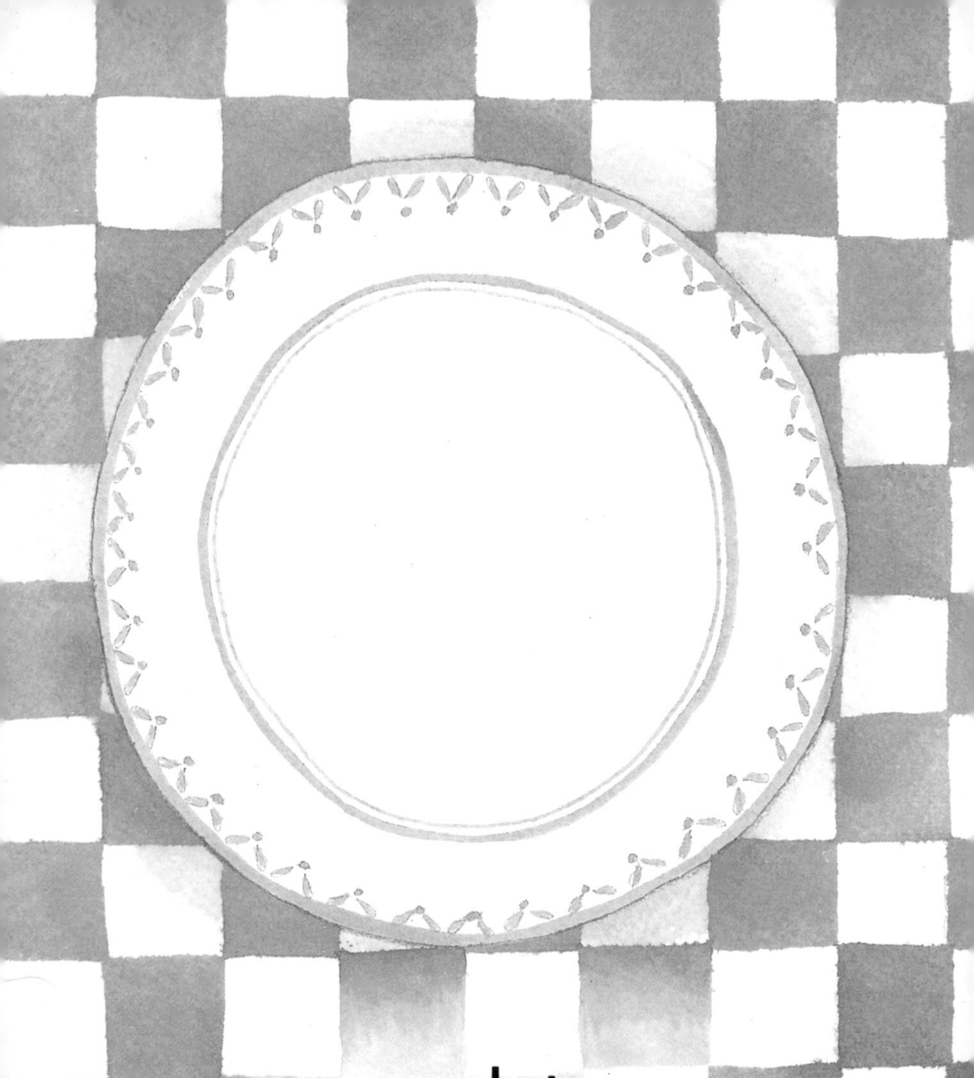

a plate,

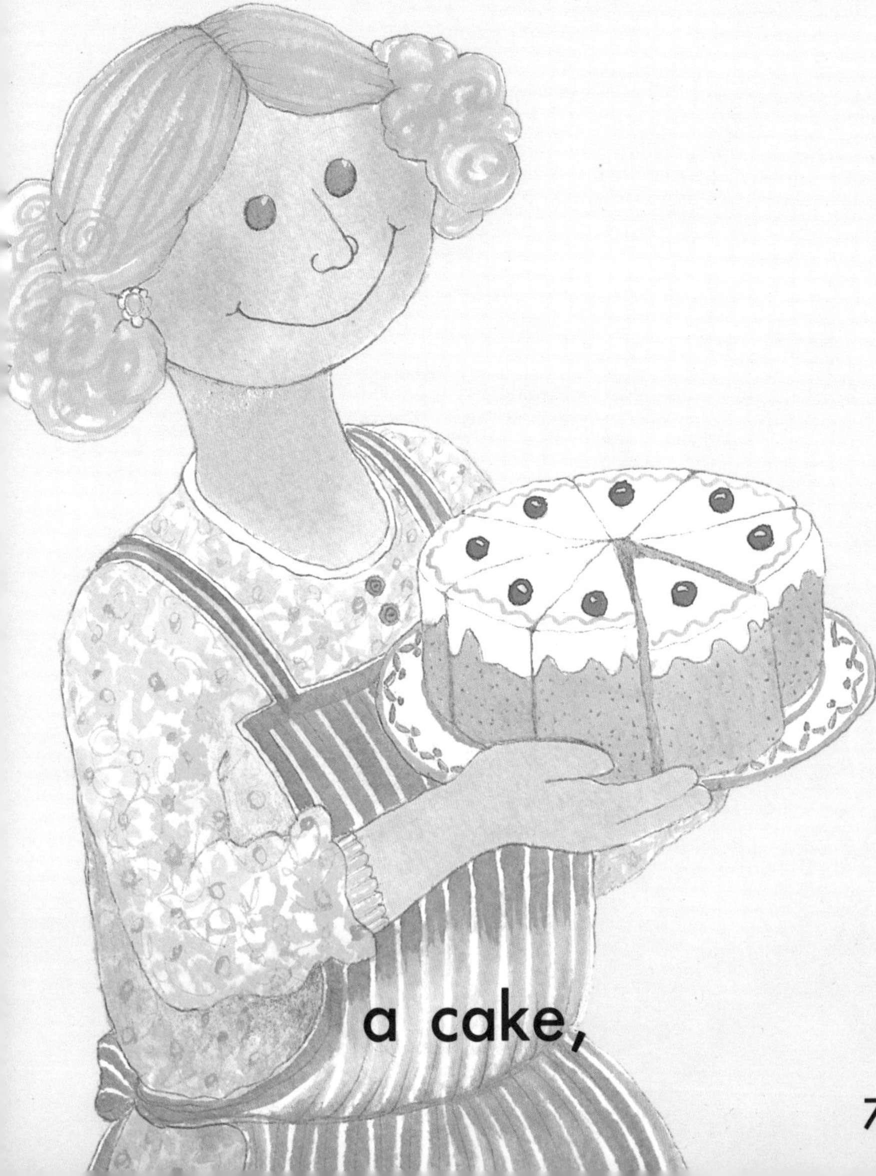

a cake,

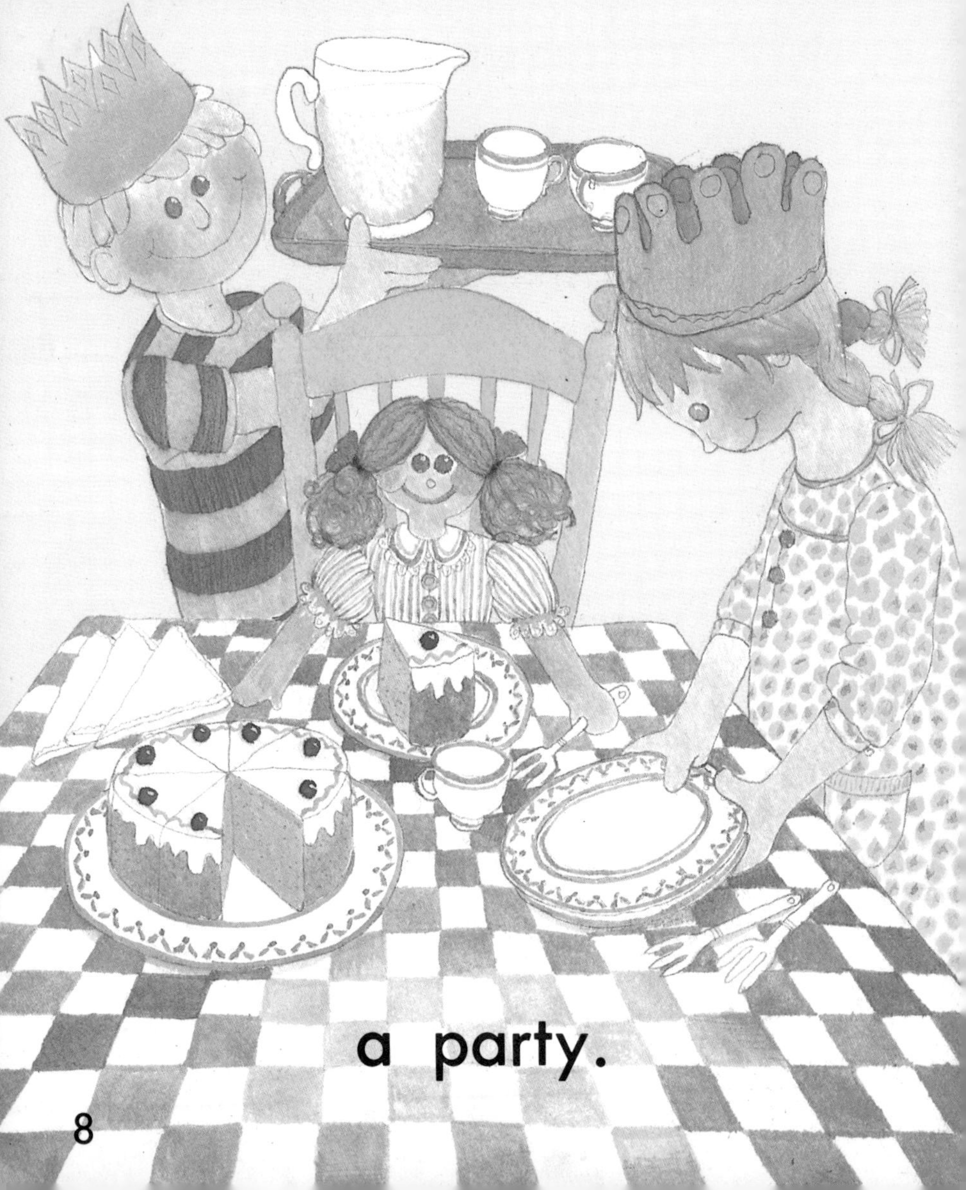

a party.